W9-CPE-983

MAY   2012

3210 41st Street

Moline Public Library

Moline, IL 61265

NBA CHAMPIONS PHILADELPHIA 76ERS

NBA CHAMPIONS

PHILADELPHIA 76ERS

AARON FRISCH

CREATIVE EDUCATION

3 0067 00005 5106

Published by Creative Education
P.O. Box 227, Mankato, Minnesota 56002
Creative Education is an imprint of The Creative Company
www.thecreativecompany.us

Book and cover design by Blue Design (www.bluedes.com)
Art direction by Rita Marshall
Printed by Corporate Graphics in the United States of
America

Photographs by Corbis (Steve Lipofsky), Getty Images
(Kim Blaxland, Focus On Sport, Jesse D. Garrabrant/NBAE,
Drew Hallowell, Walter Iooss Jr./NBAE, Neil Leifer/NBAE,
Manny Millan/Sports Illustrated, Peter Read Miller/Sports
Illustrated, NBA Photo Library/NBAE, Dick Raphael/Sports
Illustrated, John G. Zimmerman/Time & Life Pictures)

Copyright © 2012 Creative Education
International copyright reserved in all countries. No part of
this book may be reproduced in any form without written
permission from the publisher.

Library of Congress Cataloging-in-Publication Data

Frisch, Aaron.
Philadelphia 76ers / by Aaron Frisch.
p. cm. — (NBA champions)
Includes bibliographical references and index.
Summary: A basic introduction to the Philadelphia 76ers
professional basketball team, including its formation as the
Syracuse Nationals in 1949, greatest players, championships,
and stars of today.
ISBN 978-1-60818-140-7
1. Philadelphia 76ers (Basketball team)—History—Juvenile
literature. I. Title. II. Series.

GV885.52.P45F75 2012
796.323'640974811—dc22   2010052756

CPSIA: 030111 PO1448

First edition
9 8 7 6 5 4 3 2 1

Cover: Andre Iguodala
Page 2: Samuel Dalembert
Right: Billy Cunningham
Page 6: Andre Iguodala

TABLE OF CONTENTS

The 76ers have been playing in Philadelphia since 1963

Philadelphia is a city in Pennsylvania. Philadelphia is sometimes called "Philly" for short. It was one of the first large cities in the United States. Philadelphia has an **arena** called The Spectrum that is the home of a basketball team called the 76ers.

Philadelphia is nicknamed "The City of Brotherly Love"

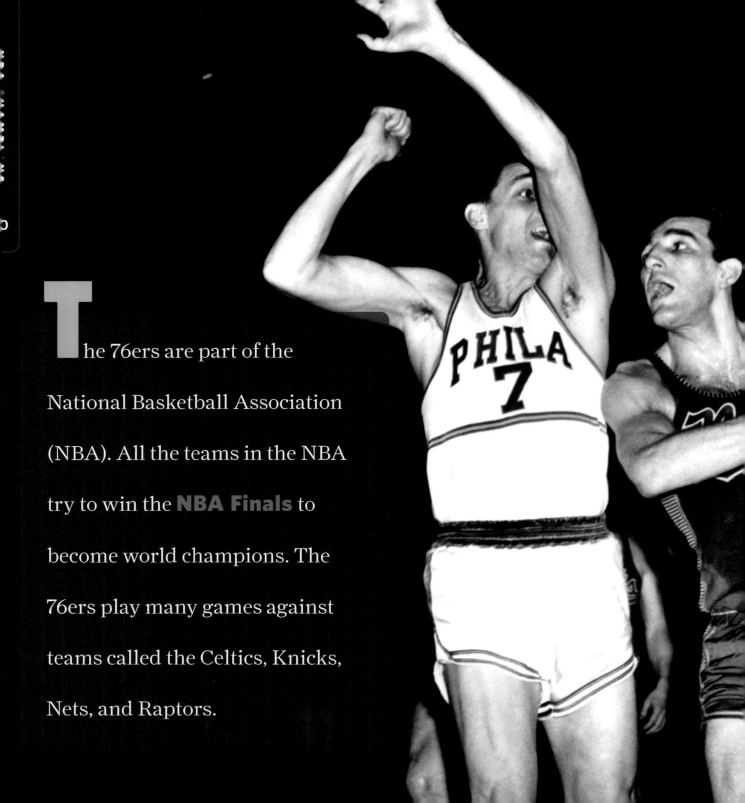

The 76ers are part of the National Basketball Association (NBA). All the teams in the NBA try to win the **NBA Finals** to become world champions. The 76ers play many games against teams called the Celtics, Knicks, Nets, and Raptors.

Dolph Schayes

The 76ers started playing in 1949. They played in Syracuse, New York, then and were called the Nationals. Players like **versatile** forward/ center Dolph Schayes made the Nationals a tough team. In 1955, they won the NBA championship.

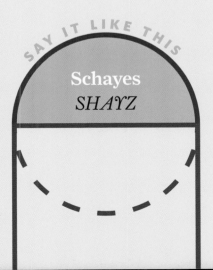

SAY IT LIKE THIS

Schayes
SHAYZ

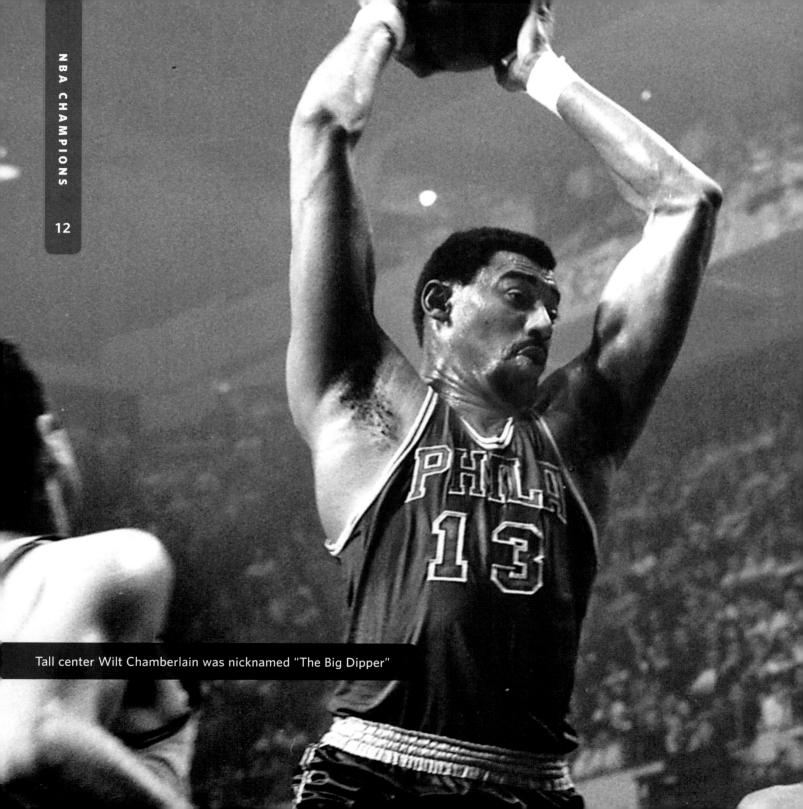

Tall center Wilt Chamberlain was nicknamed "The Big Dipper"

Why Are They Called the 76ers?
The number 76 is short for 1776. In 1776, people met in Philadelphia and decided that the United States should be its own country. Americans then fought a war against soldiers from Great Britain to be free.

In 1963, the Nationals turned into the Philadelphia 76ers. Four years later, famous center Wilt Chamberlain helped the 76ers win the 1967 NBA Finals!

76ERS FACTS

- **Started playing:** 1949 (as the Syracuse Nationals)
- **Conference/division:** Eastern Conference, Western Division
- **Team colors:** red, blue, and white
- **NBA championships:**

  1955 — 4 games to 3 versus Fort Wayne Pistons

  1967 — 4 games to 2 versus San Francisco Warriors

  1983 — 4 games to 0 versus Los Angeles Lakers
- **NBA Web site for kids:** http://www.nba.com/kids/

The 76ers had some bad seasons after that. In 1973, they ended with just 9 wins and 73 losses! But Philadelphia was soon a **contender** again. The 76ers got to the NBA Finals in 1977, 1980, and 1982 but lost every time.

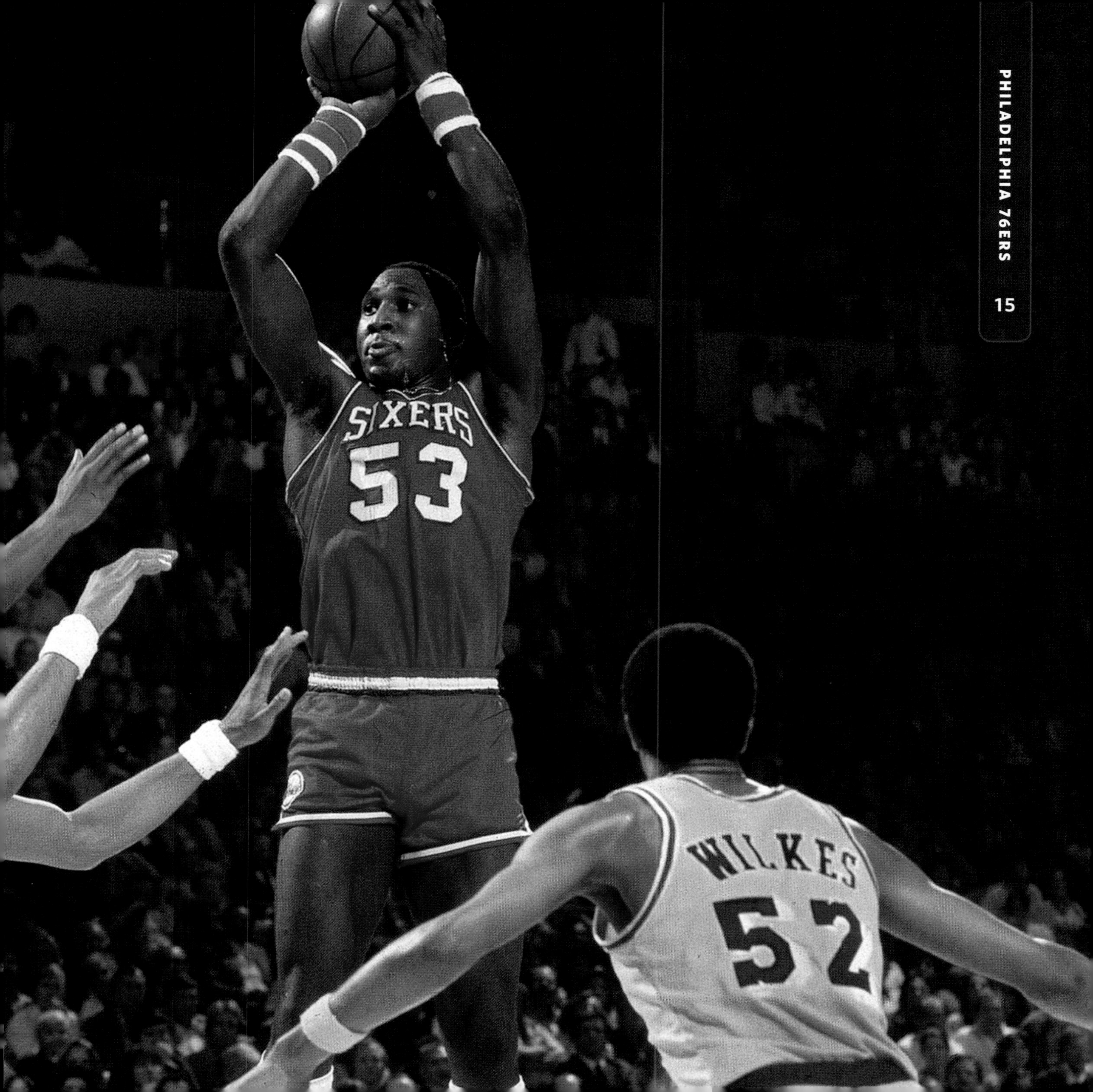
SIXERS
53
WILKES
52

Moses Malone played for the 76ers and six other NBA teams

In 1983, big center Moses Malone led the 76ers to another championship. Philadelphia celebrated with a big parade through the streets. The 76ers played well after that, but they could not win any more trophies.

76ers stars Julius Erving (above) and Hal Greer (opposite)

T he 76ers have had many stars. Hal Greer was a swingman who played for the Nationals and 76ers for 15 seasons. Julius Erving was a forward who could leap high for thrilling slam dunks. Fans called him "Dr. J."

Allen Iverson was small, but he was very quick and tough

Charles Barkley joined the 76ers in 1984. He was a powerful forward who played in the NBA **All-Star Game** 11 years in a row. Fast point guard Allen Iverson won an award as the NBA's best player in 2001.

Charles Barkley was one of the NBA's strongest rebounders

Evan Turner helped the 76ers win 41 games his first season

In 2010, the 76ers added Evan Turner. He was a tall guard with a good jump shot. Philadelphia fans hoped that he would help lead the 76ers to their fourth NBA championship!

GLOSSARY

All-Star Game — a special game in the middle of the season that only the best players get to play

arena — a large building for indoor sports events; it has many seats for fans

contender — a team that has a good chance of winning the championship

NBA Finals — a series of games between two teams at the end of the playoffs; the first team to win four games is the champion

swingman — a basketball player who can play as a guard or forward

versatile — able to do many different things well

INDEX